# A
# DIFFICULT
# SPELLING

## BOOK FOR SMART KIDS

410 Words With 6 Difficulty Levels

AGES
9-12

**Two Little Ravens**
CHILDREN'S NON-FICTION BOOKS

Paperback Edition: 9781960320452
Hardcover Edition: 9781960320469
Digital Edition: 9781960320476

Published in the United States by Two Ravens Books LLC,

254 Chapman Rd, Ste 209, Newark DE 19702

'Expand the mind, free the imagination, one title at a time.'
**www.tworavensbooks.com**

# INTROTDUCTION

Welcome to *"A Difficult Spelling Book For Smart Kids,"* a guide designed to hone the spelling skills of young learners ages 9-12.

This book contains 410 words, with a difficulty level ranging from 5 to 10.

This unique level system allows children to begin with simpler words and gradually confront more complex spellings. This progressive approach helps to steadily enhance their spelling skills, facilitating a robust improvement in their ability to spell and understand advanced vocabulary.

Expect an enriching linguistic journey that fosters progress and confidence in every young reader.

# This Book Belongs To:

_____

_____

_____

The spelling challenge begins NOW!

# TABLE OF CONTENTS

| | Page |
|---|---|

# LEVEL 5

●●●●●○○○○○

- **Abundant** a·bun·dant (adjective)
  Existing or available in large quantities; plentiful.

- **Accompany** ac·com·pa·ny (verb)
  Go somewhere with (someone) as a companion or escort.

- **Believe** be·lieve (verb)
  Accept that (something) is true, especially without proof.

- **Blemish** blem·ish (noun)
  A small mark or flaw which spoils the appearance of something.

- **Blossom** blos·som (noun)
  A flower or a mass of flowers on a tree or bush.

- **Boundary** bound·a·ry (noun)
  A line that marks the limits of an area.

- **Capture** cap·ture (verb)
  Take into one's possession or control by force.

- **Cautious** cau·tious (adjective)
  Careful to avoid potential problems or dangers.

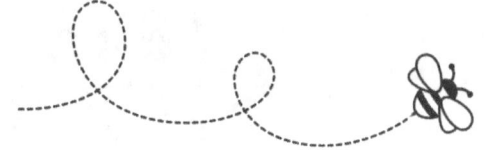

- **Consequence** con·se·quence (noun)
  A result or effect of an action or condition.

- **Curious** cu·ri·ous (adjective)
  Eager to know or learn something.

- **Delicate** del·i·cate (adjective)
  Very fine in texture or structure; of intricate workmanship or quality.

- **Determine** de·ter·mine (verb)
  Cause (something) to occur in a particular way or to have a particular nature.

- **Discrepancy** dis·crep·an·cy (noun)
  A lack of compatibility or similarity between two or more facts.

- **Diverse** di·verse (adjective)
  Showing a great deal of variety; very different.

- **Effort** ef·fort (noun)
  A vigorous or determined attempt.

- **Elevate** el·e·vate (verb)
  Raise or lift (something) to a higher position.

# LEVEL 5

●●●●●○○○○○

- **Exhibition** ex·hi·bi·tion (noun)
  A public display of works of art or items of interest.

- **Expand** ex·pand (verb)
  Become or make larger or more extensive.

- **Familiar** fa·mil·iar (adjective)
  Well known from long or close association.

- **Forgive** for·give (verb)
  Stop feeling angry or resentful toward (someone)
  for an offense, flaw, or mistake.

- **Freedom** free·dom (noun)
  The power or right to act, speak, or think as one
  wants without hindrance or restraint.

- **Frustration** frus·tra·tion (noun)
  The feeling of being upset or annoyed as a result of
  being unable to change or achieve something.

- **Genuine** gen·u·ine (adjective)
  Truly what something is said to be; authentic.

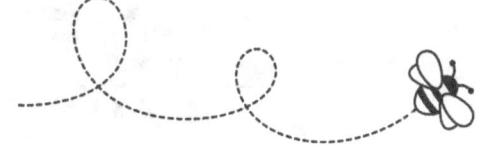

- **Glimpse** glimpse (verb)
  See or perceive briefly or partially.

- **Gradual** grad·u·al (adjective)
  Taking place or progressing slowly or by degrees.

- **Grammar** gram·mar (noun)
  The whole system and structure of a language.

- **Harmony** har·mo·ny (noun)
  The combination of simultaneously sounded musical notes to produce a pleasing effect.

- **Heritage** her·i·tage (noun)
  Valued objects and qualities such as cultural traditions, unspoiled countryside, and historic buildings.

- **Humble** hum·ble (adjective)
  Having or showing a modest or low estimate of one's own importance.

- **Humorous** hu·mor·ous (adjective)
  Funny, or making you laugh.

- **Innovate** in·no·vate (verb)
  Make changes in something established, especially by introducing new methods, ideas, or products.

- **Intelligent** in·tel·li·gent (adjective)
  Having or showing intelligence, especially of a high level.

- **Involve** in·volve (verb)
  Have or include (something) as a necessary or integral part or result.

- **Journey** jour·ney (noun)
  An act of traveling from one place to another.

- **Jovial** jo·vi·al (adjective)
  Cheerful and friendly.

- **Jubilation** ju·bi·la·tion (noun)
  A feeling of great happiness and triumph.

- **Juggle** jug·gle (verb)
  Continuously toss into the air and catch (a number of objects) so as to keep at least one in the air while handling the others.

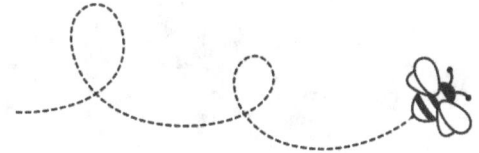

- **Kaleidoscope** ka·lei·do·scope (noun)
  A constantly changing pattern or sequence of elements.

- **Kitchen** kitch·en (noun)
  A room or area where food is prepared and cooked.

- **Kneel** kneel (verb)
  Be in or assume a position in which the body is supported by a knee on the ground.

- **Leisure** lei·sure (noun)
  Free time.

- **Lesson** les·son (noun)
  An amount of teaching given at one time.

- **Magnitude** mag·ni·tude (noun)
  The great size or extent of something.

- **Mature** ma·ture (adjective)
  Fully developed physically; full-grown.

# LEVEL 5

- **Navigate** nav·i·gate (verb)
  Plan and direct the route or course of a ship, aircraft, or other form of transportation, especially by using instruments or maps.

- **Notice** no·tice (verb)
  Become aware of.

- **Objective** ob·jec·tive (noun)
  A thing aimed at or sought; a goal.

- **Operate** op·er·ate (verb)
  Control the functioning of (a machine, process, or system).

- **Patience** pa·tience (noun)
  The capacity to accept or tolerate delay, problems, or suffering without becoming annoyed or anxious.

- **Pursue** pur·sue (verb)
  Follow or chase (someone or something).

- **Quaint** quaint (adjective)
  Attractively unusual or old-fashioned.

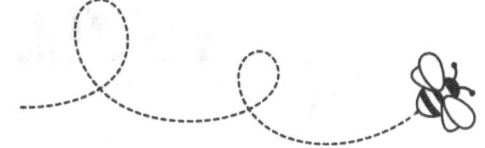

- **Quantity** quan·ti·ty (noun)
  The amount or number of a material or immaterial thing not usually estimated by spatial measurement.

- **Resolve** re·solve (verb)
  Settle or find a solution to (a problem or contentious matter).

- **Respect** re·spect (verb)
  Admire (someone or something) deeply, as a result of their abilities, qualities, or achievements.

- **Sincere** sin·cere (adjective)
  Free from pretense or deceit; proceeding from genuine feelings.

- **Subtle** sub·tle (adjective)
  So delicate or precise as to be difficult to analyze or describe.

- **Treasure** treas·ure (noun)
  A quantity of precious metals, gems, or other valuable objects.

# LEVEL 5

●●●●● ○○○○○

- **Trivial** triv·i·al (adjective)
  Of little value or importance.

- **Umbrella** um·brel·la (noun)
  A device consisting of a circular canopy of cloth on a folding frame supported by a central rod, used as protection against rain or sometimes sun.

- **Unique** u·nique (adjective)
  Being the only one of its kind; unlike anything else.

- **Victory** vic·to·ry (noun)
  An act of defeating an enemy or opponent in a battle, game, or other competition.

- **Viol** viol (noun)
  A musical stringed instrument of the Renaissance and Baroque periods.

- **Volume** vol·ume (noun)
  The amount of space that a substance or object occupies, or that is enclosed within a container.

- **Whorl** whorl (noun)
  A pattern of spirals or concentric circles.

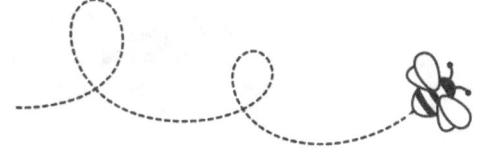

- **Witness** wit·ness (noun)
  A person who sees an event, typically a crime or accident, take place.

- **Xerox** xe·rox (verb)
  Make a copy with a xerographic copier; (noun) a photocopy.

- **Yield** yield (verb)
  Produce or provide (a natural, agricultural, or industrial product).

- **Youthful** youth·ful (adjective)
  Having the characteristics of youth; young or seeming young.

- **Zealous** zeal·ous (adjective)
  Having or showing zeal; fervent.

- **Zodiac** zo·di·ac (noun)
  A belt of the heavens within about 8° either side of the ecliptic, including all apparent positions of the sun, moon, and most familiar planets.

# LEVEL 6

- **Accommodate** ac·com·mo·date (verb)
  Provide lodging or sufficient space for.

- **Alacrity** alac·ri·ty (noun)
  Brisk and cheerful readiness.

- **Alleviate** al·le·vi·ate (verb)
  Make (suffering, deficiency, or a problem) less severe.

- **Amplify** am·pli·fy (verb)
  Increase the volume of (sound).

- **Biodegradable** bio·de·grad·a·ble (adjective)
  Capable of being decomposed by bacteria or other living organisms.

- **Blatant** bla·tant (adjective)
  Done openly and unashamedly.

- **Cognition** cog·ni·tion (noun)
  The mental action or process of acquiring knowledge and understanding through thought.

- **Colloquium** col·lo·qui·um (noun)
  An academic conference or seminar.

- **Combustible** com·bus·ti·ble (adjective)
  Able to catch fire and burn easily.

- **Commemorate** com·mem·o·rate (verb)
  Recall and show respect for (someone or
  something) in a ceremony.

- **Compartmentalize** com·part·men·tal·ize (verb)
  Divide into sections or categories.

- **Complicit** com·plic·it (adjective)
  Involved with others in an illegal activity or
  wrongdoing.

- **Construe** con·strue (verb)
  Interpret (a word or action) in a particular way.

- **Detrimental** det·ri·men·tal (adjective)
  Tending to cause harm.

- **Disintegrate** dis·in·te·grate (verb)
  Break up into small parts, typically as the result of
  impact or decay.

- **Eccentricity** ec·cen·tric·i·ty (noun)
  The quality of being eccentric (deviating from conventional or accepted usage or conduct).

- **Exaggerate** ex·ag·ger·ate (verb)
  Represent (something) as being larger, better, or worse than it really is.

- **Fettle** fet·tle (noun)
  Condition.

- **Fictitious** fic·ti·tious (adjective)
  Not real or true; imaginary or fabricated.

- **Fledgling** fledg·ling (noun)
  A young bird that has just fledged.

- **Forbearance** for·bear·ance (noun)
  Patient self-control; restraint and tolerance.

- **Gratification** grat·i·fi·ca·tion (noun)
  Pleasure, especially when gained from the satisfaction of a desire.

- **Hypocritical** hy·po·crit·i·cal (adjective)
  Behaving in a way that suggests one has higher standards or more noble beliefs than is the case.

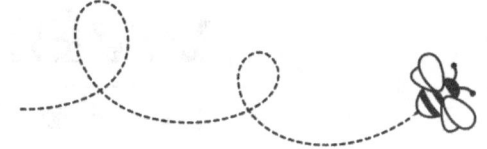

- **Impersonate** im·per·son·ate (verb)
  Pretend to be (another person) for entertainment or fraud.

- **Incongruous** in·con·gru·ous (adjective)
  Not in harmony or keeping with the surroundings or other aspects of something.

- **Jurisdiction** ju·ris·dic·tion (noun)
  The official power to make legal decisions and judgments.

- **Juxtaposition** jux·ta·po·si·tion (noun)
  The fact of two things being seen or placed close together with contrasting effect.

- **Kilometer** kil·o·me·ter (noun)
  A metric unit of measurement equal to 1,000 meters.

- **Kinesthetic** kin·es·thet·ic (adjective)
  Relating to a person's awareness of the position and movement of the parts of the body by means of sensory organs (proprioceptors) in the muscles and joints.

# LEVEL 6

- **Knapsack** knap·sack (noun)
  A bag carried by a strap on your back or shoulder.

- **Leverage** lev·er·age (noun)
  The exertion of force by means of a lever or an object used in the manner of a lever.

- **Liaison** li·ai·son (noun)
  Communication or cooperation that facilitates a close working relationship between people or organizations.

- **Luxurious** lux·u·ri·ous (adjective)
  Extremely comfortable or elegant, especially when involving great expense.

- **Manipulate** ma·nip·u·late (verb)
  Handle or control (a tool, mechanism, etc.), Typically in a skillful manner.

- **Misinterpret** mis·in·ter·pret (verb)
  Interpret (something or someone) wrongly.

- **Monologue** mono·logue (noun)
  A long speech by one actor in a play or movie, or as part of a theatrical or broadcast program.

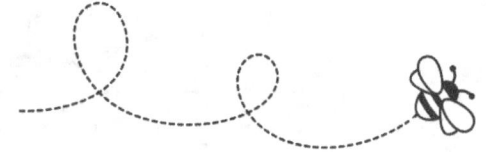

- **Monotonous** mo·not·o·nous (adjective)
  Dull, tedious, and repetitious; lacking in variety and interest.

- **Necessitate** ne·ces·si·tate (verb)
  Make (something) necessary as a result or consequence.

- **Neutralize** neu·tral·ize (verb)
  Render (something) ineffective or harmless by applying an opposite force or effect.

- **Nonchalant** non·cha·lant (adjective)
  Feeling or appearing casually calm and relaxed; not displaying anxiety, interest, or enthusiasm.

- **Obliterate** ob·lit·er·ate (verb)
  Destroy utterly; wipe out.

- **Quadrilateral** quad·ri·lat·er·al (noun)
  A four-sided figure.

- **Quintessential** quin·tes·sen·tial (adjective)
  Representing the most perfect or typical example of a quality or class.

# LEVEL 6

- **Quintuplet** quin·tu·plet (noun)
  Each of five children born to the same mother at one birth.

- **Refulgent** re·ful·gent (adjective)
  Shining brightly; radiant.

- **Reimburse** re·im·burse (verb)
  Repay (a person who has spent or lost money).

- **Resilience** re·sil·ience (noun)
  The capacity to recover quickly from difficulties; toughness.

- **Resonance** res·o·nance (noun)
  The quality in a sound of being deep, full, and reverberating.

- **Resonate** res·o·nate (verb)
  Produce or be filled with a deep, full, reverberating sound.

- **Simultaneously** si·mul·ta·ne·ous·ly (adverb)
  At the same time.

- **Surveillance** sur·veil·lance (noun)
  Close observation, especially of a suspected spy or criminal.

- **Sustainability** sus·tain·a·bil·i·ty (noun)
  The ability to be maintained at a certain rate or level.

- **Transparency** trans·par·en·cy (noun)
  The condition of being transparent.

- **Turbulence** tur·bu·lence (noun)
  Violent or unsteady movement of air or water, or of some other fluid.

- **Tyrannical** tyr·an·ni·cal (adjective)
  Exercising power in a cruel or arbitrary way.

- **Unanimous** u·nan·i·mous (adjective)
  (Of two or more people) fully in agreement.

- **Unbelievable** un·be·liev·able (adjective)
  Not able to be believed; unlikely to be true.

- **Unprecedented** un·prec·e·dent·ed (adjective)
  Never done or known before.

# LEVEL 6

- **Vaccination** vac·ci·na·tion (noun)
  Treatment with a vaccine to produce immunity against a disease.

- **Vigilant** vig·i·lant (adjective)
  Keeping careful watch for possible danger or difficulties.

- **Vulnerability** vul·ner·a·bil·i·ty (noun)
  The quality or state of being exposed to the possibility of being attacked or harmed, either physically or emotionally.

- **Waif** waif (noun)
  A homeless and helpless person, especially a neglected or abandoned child.

- **Wavelength** wave·length (noun)
  The distance between successive crests of a wave.

- **Whirligig** whirl·i·gig (noun)
  A toy that spins around, for example a top or windmill.

 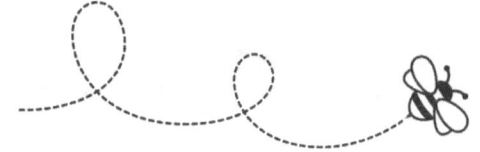

- **Wholesome** whole·some (adjective)
  Conducive to or suggestive of good health and physical well-being.

- **Xylophone** xy·lo·phone (noun)
  A musical instrument played by striking a row of wooden bars of graduated length with one or more small wooden or plastic mallets.

- **Yearning** yearn·ing (noun)
  A feeling of intense longing for something.

- **Yesteryear** yes·ter·year (noun)
  Last year or the recent past, especially as nostalgically recalled.

- **Zeppelin** zep·pe·lin (noun)
  A large german dirigible airship of the early 20th century.

- **Zoology** zo·ol·o·gy (noun)
  The scientific study of the behavior, structure, physiology, classification, and distribution of animals.

# LET'S
# LEVEL
# UP

# LEVEL 7

- **Absorbency** ab·sorb·en·cy (noun)
  The ability to soak up liquid.

- **Biodiversity** bio·di·ver·si·ty (noun)
  The variety of plant and animal life in the world or in a particular habitat.

- **Communicable** com·mu·ni·ca·ble (adjective)
  Able of being transmitted from one person or species to another.

- **Discombobulate** dis·com·bob·u·late (verb)
  Disconcert or confuse (someone).

- **Diatribe** di·a·tribe (noun)
  A forceful and bitter verbal attack.

- **Grandiloquent** gran·di·lo·quent (adjective)
  Pompous or extravagant in language, style, or manner.

- **Heterogeneous** het·er·o·ge·neous (adjective)
  Diverse in character or content.

# LEVEL 7

- **Lackadaisical** lack·a·dai·si·cal (adjective)
  Lacking enthusiasm and determination.

- **Fiacre** fi·a·cre (noun)
  A small horse-drawn carriage.

- **Mammoth** mam·moth (noun)
  A large extinct elephant of the Pleistocene epoch.

- **Maudlin** maud·lin (adjective)
  Self-pityingly or tearfully sentimental.

- **Quintessential** quin·tes·sen·tial (adjective)
  Representing the most perfect or typical example.

- **Knowledgeable** know·ledge·a·ble (adjective)
  Intelligent and well informed.

- **Thermodynamics** ther·mo·dy·nam·ics (noun)
  The branch of physical science that deals with the relations between heat and other forms of energy.

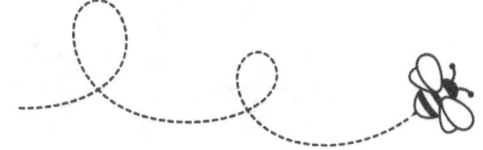

- **Imperceptible** im·per·cep·ti·ble (adjective)
  So slight, gradual, or subtle as not to be perceived.

- **Convivial** con·viv·i·al (adjective)
  Friendly, lively, and enjoyable.

- **Repercussion** rep·er·cus·sion (noun)
  An unintended consequence of an event or action.

- **Fatuous** fat·u·ous (adjective)
  Silly and pointless.

- **Xenophobia** xe·no·pho·bia (noun)
  Dislike of or prejudice against people from other countries.

- **Stereotype** ste·re·o·type (noun)
  A widely held but fixed and oversimplified image or idea of a particular type of person or thing.

- **Eclectic** e·clec·tic (adjective)
  Deriving ideas, style, or taste from a broad and diverse range of sources.

# LEVEL 7

- **Unambiguous** un·am·big·u·ous (adjective)
  Not open to more than one interpretation.

- **Reciprocate** rec·i·proc·ate (verb)
  Respond to (a gesture or action) by making a corresponding one.

- **Vindicate** vin·di·cate (verb)
  Clear (someone) of blame or suspicion.

- **Abolition** a·bol·i·tion (noun)
  The action or an act of abolishing a system, practice, or institution.

- **Bibliography** bib·li·og·ra·phy (noun)
  A list of the books referred to in a scholarly work, typically printed as an appendix.

- **Consciousness** con·scious·ness (noun)
  The state of being aware of and able to think and perceive one's surroundings, thoughts, and feelings.

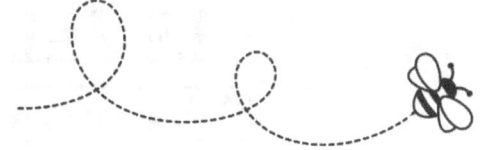

- **Dehydrate** de·hy·drate (verb)
  Cause (a person or their body) to lose a large amount of water.

- **Exhilarating** ex·hil·a·rat·ing (adjective)
  Making one feel very happy, animated, or elated; thrilling.

- **Fluctuation** fluc·tu·a·tion (noun)
  An irregular rising and falling in number or amount; a variation.

- **Geographical** ge·o·graph·i·cal (adjective)
  Relating to geography or an area of study.

- **Humanitarian** hu·man·i·tar·i·an (noun)
  A person who seeks to promote human welfare; a philanthropist.

- **Impersonal** im·per·son·al (adjective)
  Not influenced by, showing, or involving personal feelings.

# LEVEL 7

- **Justification** jus·ti·fi·ca·tion (noun)
  The action of showing something to be right or reasonable.

- **Lethargic** leth·ar·gic (adjective)
  Affected by lethargy; sluggish and apathetic.

- **Travesty** trav·es·ty (noun)
  A false, absurd, or distorted representation of something.

- **Omnipotent** om·nip·o·tent (adjective)
  Having unlimited power; able to do anything.

- **Paradigm** par·a·digm (noun)
  A typical example or pattern of something; a model.

- **Reconciliation** rec·on·cil·i·a·tion (noun)
  The restoration of friendly relations.

- **Stigmatize** stig·ma·tize (verb)
  Describe or regard as worthy of disgrace or great disapproval.

- **Translucent** trans·lu·cent (adjective)
  Allowing light, but not detailed shapes, to pass through; semi-transparent.

- **Unparalleled** un·par·al·leled (adjective)
  Having no parallel or equal; exceptional.

- **Vociferous** vo·cif·er·ous (adjective)
  Vehement or clamorous.

- **Megalopolis** meg·a·lop·o·lis (noun)
  A very large, heavily populated city or urban complex.

- **Inquisitive** in·quis·i·tive (adjective)
  Curious or inquiring.

- **Commingle** com·min·gle (verb)
  Mix; blend.

- **Firkin** fir·kin (noun)
  A small cask.

# LEVEL 7

- **Labyrinth** lab·y·rinth (noun)
  A complicated irregular network of passages or paths in which it is difficult to find one's way; a maze.

- **Metamorphosis** met·a·mor·pho·sis (noun)
  A change of the form or nature of a thing or person into a completely different one.

- **Nomenclature** no·men·cla·ture (noun)
  The devising or choosing of names for things, especially in a science or other discipline.

- **Omniscient** om·nis·cient (adjective)
  Knowing everything.

- **Paraphernalia** par·a·pher·na·lia (noun)
  Miscellaneous articles, especially the equipment needed for a particular activity.

- **Quintillion** quin·til·lion (noun)
  A cardinal number represented in the u.S. By 1 followed by 18 zeros, and in great britain by 1 followed by 30 zeros.

- **Aberration** ab·er·ra·tion (noun)
  A departure from what is normal, usual, or expected, typically an unwelcome one.

- **Sophisticate** so·phis·ti·cate (verb)
  Make (someone or something) more sophisticated.

- **Thermoelasticity** ther·mo·e·las·tic·i·ty (noun)
  The property of certain materials to change their shape in response to changes in temperature.

- **Unidimensionality** u·ni·di·men·sion·al·i·ty (noun)
  The quality of being measurable in only one dimension.

- **Ubiquitous** u·biq·ui·tous (adjective)
  present, appearing, or found everywhere.

- **Vasoconstriction** va·so·con·stric·tion (noun)
  The constriction of blood vessels, which increases blood pressure.

- **Circumscribe** cir·cum·scribe (verb)
  Restrict (something) within limits.

- **Expunge** ex·punge (verb)
  Erase or remove completely.

- **Zootechnics** zo·o·tech·nics (noun)
  The science of breeding and tending domestic animals.

- **Refrigeration** re·frig·er·a·tion (noun)
  The process of causing or maintaining the cooling of a space, substance, or system.

- **Regalia** re·gal·ia (noun)
  The emblems or insignia of royalty.

- **Circumlocutory** cir·cum·loc·u·to·ry (adjective)
  Speaking or writing in a roundabout or indirect way.

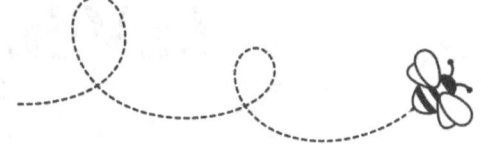

- **Dextrocardia** dex·tro·car·di·a (noun)
  A rare congenital condition where the heart is situated on the right side of the body.

- **Visage** vi·sage (noun)
  A person's face, with reference to the form or proportions of the features.

- **Kindheartedness** kind·heart·ed·ness (noun)
  The quality of being friendly, generous, and considerate.

## Bonus Words:

- **Penchant** pen·chant (noun)
  A strong or habitual liking for something or tendency to do something.

- **Winebibber** wine·bib·ber (noun)
  A person who drinks a lot of wine.

# LEVEL 8

- **Apprehension** ap·pre·hen·sion (noun)
  Anxiety or fear that something bad or unpleasant will happen.

- **Bureaucracy** bu·reau·cra·cy (noun)
  A system of government in which most of the important decisions are made by state officials.

- **Flambeau** flam·beau (noun)
  A flaming torch.

- **Deterioration** de·te·ri·o·ra·tion (noun)
  The process of becoming progressively worse.

- **Exemplification** ex·em·pli·fi·ca·tion (noun)
  A representative example or case.

- **Fluorescent** fluo·res·cent (adjective)
  The emission of light by a substance that has absorbed light or other electromagnetic radiation.

- **Festschrift** fest·schrift (noun)
  A collection of writings published in honor of a scholar.

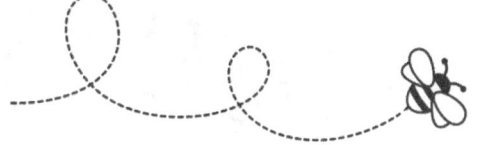

- **Hyperbolic** hy·per·bol·ic (adjective)
  Relating to a hyperbola or exaggerated.

- **Inconsequential** in·con·se·quen·tial (adjective)
  Not important or significant.

- **Belligerent** bel·lig·er·ent (adjective)
  Hostile and aggressive.

- **Malignant** ma·lig·nant (adjective)
  Very virulent or infectious.

- **Malodorous** mal·o·dor·ous (adjective)
  Smelling very unpleasant.

- **Megalith** meg·a·lith (noun)
  A large stone that has been used to construct a
  structure or monument.

- **Neuroscience** neu·ro·sci·ence (noun)
  Any or all of the sciences, such as neurochemistry
  and experimental psychology, which deal with
  the structure or function of the nervous system and
  brain.

# LEVEL 8

- **Ophthalmologist** oph·thal·mol·o·gist (noun)
  A specialist in the branch of medicine concerned with the study and treatment of disorders and diseases of the eye.

- **Petrichor** pet·ri·chor (noun)
  A pleasant smell that frequently accompanies the first rain after a long period of warm, dry weather.

- **Quintuplet** quin·tu·plet (noun)
  Each of five children born to the same mother at one birth.

- **Rehabilitation** re·ha·bil·i·ta·tion (noun)
  The action of restoring someone to health or normal life through training and therapy.

- **Synchronization** syn·chro·ni·za·tion (noun)
  The operation or activity of two or more things at the same time or rate.

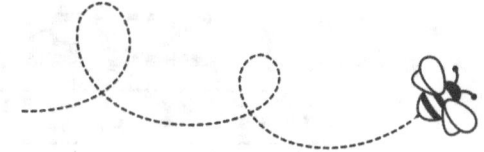

- **Thermometer** ther·mom·e·ter (noun)
  An instrument for measuring and indicating temperature.

- **Uncharacteristic** un·char·ac·ter·is·tic (adjective)
  Not typical of a particular person or thing.

- **Valedictorian** val·e·dic·to·ri·an (noun)
  A student typically having the highest academic achievements of the class.

- **Wholesaler** whole·sal·er (noun)
  A person or company that sells goods in large quantities to retailers.

- **Xylography** xy·lo·graph·y (noun)
  The art of engraving on wood.

- **Dodecahedron** do·dec·a·he·dron (noun)
  A three-dimensional shape having twelve plane faces, in particular a regular solid figure with twelve equal pentagonal faces.

# LEVEL 8

- **Yachtsman** yacht·sman (noun)
  A person who owns or sails a yacht.

- **Zoogeography** zoo·ge·og·ra·phy (noun)
  The geographical distribution of animals.

- **Empirical** em·pir·i·cal (adjective)
  Based on, concerned with, or verifiable by observation or experience rather than theory or pure logic.

- **Polyglot** poly·glot (noun)
  A person who knows and is able to use several languages.

- **Cartography** car·tog·ra·phy (noun)
  The science or practice of drawing maps.

- **Circumference** cir·cum·fer·ence (noun)
  The enclosing boundary of a curved geometric figure, especially a circle.

- **Rapporteur** rap·por·teur (noun)
  A person who is appointed by an organization to report on the proceedings of its meetings.

- **Extrapolate** ex·trap·o·late (verb)
  Extend the application of (a method or conclusion) to an unknown situation by assuming that existing trends will continue or similar methods will be applicable.

- **Gerontology** ger·on·tol·o·gy (noun)
  The scientific study of old age, the process of aging, and the particular problems of old people.

- **Hemoglobin** he·mo·glo·bin (noun)
  A red protein responsible for transporting oxygen in the blood of vertebrates.

- **Iconoclast** icon·o·clast (noun)
  A person who attacks cherished beliefs or institutions.

- **Malcontent** mal·con·tent (noun)
  A person who is dissatisfied and rebellious.

- **Kilobyte** ki·lo·byte (noun)
  A unit of memory or data equal to 1,024 (210) bytes.

# LEVEL 8

- **Lymphocyte** lymph·o·cyte (noun)
  A form of small leukocyte (white blood cell) with a single round nucleus, occurring especially in the lymphatic system.

- **Myrmidon** myr·mi·don (noun)
  A loyal follower, especially one who executes orders without question.

- **Necromancy** nec·ro·man·cy (noun)
  The supposed practice of communicating with the dead, especially in order to predict the future.

- **Oligarchy** ol·i·gar·chy (noun)
  A small group of people having control of a country or organization.

- **Blandishment** blan·dish·ment (noun)
  A flattering or pleasing statement or action used to persuade someone gently to do something.

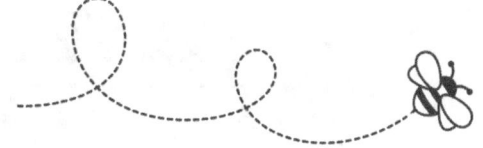

- **Quasar** qua·sar (noun)
  A massive and extremely remote celestial object, emitting exceptionally large amounts of energy.

- **Commensurate** com·men·su·rate (adjective)
  Corresponding in size or degree; in proportion.

- **Serendipity** ser·en·dip·i·ty (noun)
  The occurrence and development of events by chance in a happy or beneficial way.

- **Ultraviolet** ul·tra·vi·o·let (adjective)
  Having a wavelength shorter than that of the violet end of the visible spectrum but longer than that of X-rays.

- **Vexillology** vex·il·lol·o·gy (noun)
  The study of flags.

- **Whistleblower** whis·tle·blow·er (noun)
  A person who informs on a person or organization regarded as engaging in an unlawful or immoral activity.

- **Ameliorate** ame·lio·rate (verb)
  Make (something bad or unsatisfactory) better.

- **Zephyr** zeph·yr (noun)
  A soft gentle breeze.

- **Maelstrom** mael·strom (noun)
  A powerful whirlpool in the sea or a river.

- **Deconstruct** de·con·struct (verb)
  Analyze (a text or a linguistic or conceptual system) by deconstruction, typically in order to expose its hidden internal assumptions and contradictions and subvert its apparent significance or unity.

 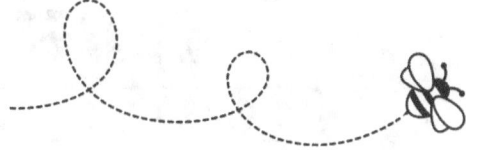

- **Coalesce** co·a·lesce (verb)
  Come together to form one mass or whole.

- **Embezzlement** em·bez·zle·ment (noun)
  Theft or misappropriation of funds placed in one's trust or belonging to one's employer.

- **Ferromagnetic** fer·ro·mag·net·ic (adjective)
  Relating to matter with strong magnetic properties.

- **Gravitation** grav·i·ta·tion (noun)
  Movement, or the tendency to move, towards a centre of gravity.

- **Hemorrhage** hem·or·rhage (noun)
  An escape of blood from a ruptured blood vessel.

# LEVEL 8

●●●●●●●●●○○

- **Verbose** ver·bose (adjective)
  Using or expressed in more words than are needed.

- **Kinetoscope** kin·e·to·scope (noun)
  An early motion-picture device in which the images were viewed through a peephole.

- **Lymphoma** lymph·o·ma (noun)
  Cancer of the lymph nodes.

- **Myocardium** my·o·car·di·um (noun)
  The muscular tissue of the heart.

- **Neuropathy** neu·rop·a·thy (noun)
  Disease or dysfunction of one or more peripheral nerves, typically causing numbness or weakness.

- **Mendicant** men·di·cant (noun)
  A beggar.

- **Quadrilateral** quad·ri·lat·er·al (noun)
  A four-sided figure.

- **Recumbent** re·cum·bent (adjective)
  Lying down.

- **Synergy** syn·er·gy (noun)
  The interaction or cooperation of two or more organizations, substances, or other agents.

- **Kinaesthetically** ki·naes·thet·i·cal·ly (adverb)
  In a way that relates to the perception of the movement and position of our bodies.

## Bonus Words:

- **Misidentification**
  mis·i·den·ti·fi·ca·tion (noun)
  Incorrect identification of someone or something.

- **Nonjusticiable** non·jus·ti·ci·a·ble (adjective)
  Not subject to trial in a court of law.

# LEVEL 9

- **Pejorative** pe·jo·ra·tive (adjective)
  Expressing contempt or disapproval.

- **Misanthrope** mis·an·thrope (noun)
  A person who dislikes humankind and avoids human society.

- **Lexicographical** lex·i·co·graph·i·cal (adjective)
  Relating to the practice of compiling dictionaries.

- **Disproportionateness**
  dis·pro·por·tion·ate·ness (noun)
  The quality or condition of being out of proportion.

- **Ecclesiastically** ec·cle·si·as·ti·cal·ly (adverb)
  In a way that relates to the Christian Church or its clergy.

- **Fluoridation** flu·or·i·da·tion (noun)
  The process of adding fluoride to the water supply of a community to reduce tooth decay.

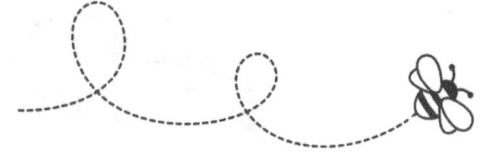

- **Hydroelectricity** hy·dro·e·lec·tric·i·ty (noun)
  Electricity produced from generators that are driven
  by moving water.

- **Inconceivability** in·con·ceiv·a·bil·i·ty (noun)
  The state of being impossible to imagine or
  comprehend.

- **Jurisprudence** ju·ris·pru·dence (noun)
  The theory or philosophy of law.

- **Lactobacillus** lac·to·ba·cil·lus (noun)
  A bacterium which produces lactic acid, especially
  in the fermentation of carbohydrates.

- **Meningococcal** men·in·go·coc·cal (adjective)
  Of or relating to the meningococcus bacteria.

- **Noncommunicable**
  non·com·mu·ni·ca·ble (adjective)
  (of a disease) Not able to be transmitted from one
  person to another.

# LEVEL 9

- **Phenylketonuria** phen·yl·ke·to·nu·ri·a (noun)
  A hereditary condition that affects the metabolism of the amino acid phenylalanine.

- **Quadruplicity** quad·ru·plic·i·ty (noun)
  The state of being fourfold or the fact of occurring four times.

- **Unconstitutional** un·con·sti·tu·tion·al (adjective)
  Not in accordance with a political constitution, especially the US Constitution, or with procedural rules.

- **Regisseur** re·gis·seur (noun)
  A person who stages a theatrical production.

- **Gargantuan** gar·gan·tu·an (adjective)
  Enormous.

- **Recalcitrant** re·cal·ci·trant (adjective)
  Having an obstinately uncooperative attitude toward authority or discipline.

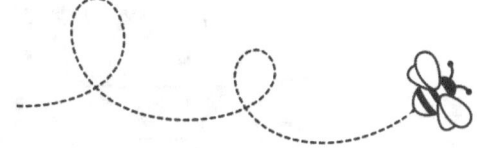

- **Idiosyncratic** id·i·o·syn·crat·ic (adjective)
  Pertaining to the nature of idiosyncrasy, or something peculiar to an individual.

- **Acknowledgment** ac·knowl·edg·ment (noun)
  The act of acknowledging; recognition or favorable notice of an act or achievement.

- **Diaphanous** di·aph·a·nous (adjective)
  Light, delicate, and translucent.

- **Constitutionality** con·sti·tu·tion·al·i·ty (noun)
  The quality of being in accordance with a political constitution.

- **Disenfranchisement**
  dis·en·fran·chise·ment (noun)
  The state of being deprived of a right or privilege, especially the right to vote.

- **Egregious** e·gre·gious (adjective)
  Outstandingly bad; shocking.

# LEVEL 9

- **Electrocardiography**
e·lec·tro·car·di·og·ra·phy (noun)
The recording and study of the electrical activity of the heart.

- **Geotropism** geo·trop·ism (noun)
The growth or movement of a plant or animal in response to gravity.

- **Hydrodynamics** hy·dro·dy·nam·ics (noun)
The branch of physics that deals with the motion of fluids and the forces acting on solid bodies immersed in fluids and in motion relative to them.

- **Immateriality** im·ma·te·ri·al·i·ty (noun)
The state or quality of being immaterial or unimportant.

- **Interlocutor** in·ter·loc·u·tor (noun)
A person who takes part in a dialogue or conversation.

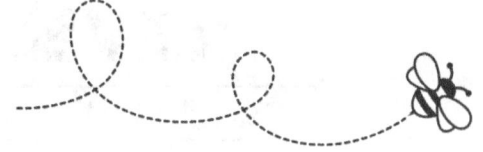

- **Legerdemain** le·ger·de·main (noun)
  Skillful use of one's hands when performing conjuring tricks.

- **Mendacious** men·da·cious (adjective)
  Not telling the truth; lying.

- **Megalomaniacal** meg·a·lo·ma·ni·a·cal (adjective)
  Having a pathological obsession with grandiose or extravagant things or actions.

- **Nonconformity** non·con·for·mi·ty (noun)
  Failure or refusal to conform to a prevailing rule or practice.

- **Obstreperous** ob·strep·er·ous (adjective)
  Noisy and difficult to control.

- **Photosensitivity** pho·to·sen·si·tiv·i·ty (noun)
  Having an extreme sensitivity to light.

# LEVEL 9

- **Anagnorisis** anag·no·ri·sis (noun)
The moment in a play or other work when a character makes a critical discovery.

- **Coruscant** co·rus·cant (adjective)
Glittering; sparkling.

- **Stereotypical** ste·re·o·typ·i·cal (adjective)
Lacking originality or individuality; conventional.

- **Supercilious** su·per·cil·i·ous (adjective)
Behaving or looking as though one thinks one is superior to others.

- **Penurious** pe·nu·ri·ous (adjective)
Extremely poor; poverty-stricken.

- **Ventriloquism** ven·tril·o·quism (noun)
The art or practice of speaking, with little or no lip movement, in such a manner that the voice does not appear to come from the speaker but from another source.

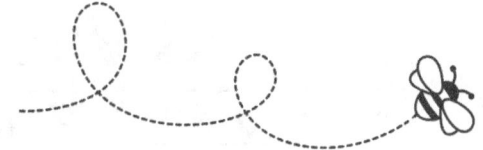

- **Whippersnapper** whip·per·snap·per (noun)
  A young and inexperienced person considered to be presumptuous or overconfident.

- **Predilection** pre·di·lec·tion (noun)
  A preference or special liking for something; a bias in favor of something.

- **Youthquake** youth·quake (noun)
  A significant cultural, political, or social change arising from the actions or influence of young people.

- **Vicissitude** vi·cis·si·tude (noun)
  A change of circumstances or fortune, typically one that is unwelcome or unpleasant.

- **Nidificate** ni·dif·i·cate (verb)
  To build a nest.

- **Valetudinarian** va·le·tu·di·nar·i·an (noun)
  A person who is unduly anxious about their health.

# LEVEL 9

●●●●●●●●●●○

- **Bourgeoisie** bour·geoi·sie (noun)
  The middle class, typically with reference to its perceived materialistic values or conventional attitudes.

- **Chlorofluorocarbon**
  chloro·fluoro·carbon (noun)
  Any of a class of compounds of carbon, hydrogen, chlorine, and fluorine, typically gases used in refrigerants and aerosol propellants.

- **Gasconade** gas·co·nade (noun)
  Extravagant boasting.

- **Hypercholesterolemia**
  hy·per·cho·les·ter·ol·e·mi·a (noun)
  An excess of cholesterol in the bloodstream.

- **Parsimonious** par·si·mo·ni·ous (adjective)
  Unwilling to spend money or use resources; stingy or frugal.

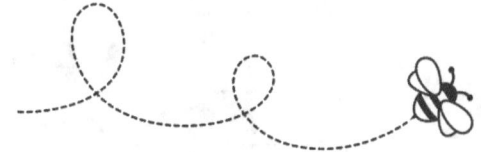

- **Meteorologist** me·te·or·ol·o·gist (noun)
  A scientist who studies or practices meteorology.

- **Quadrillion** quad·ril·lion (noun)
  The cardinal number represented as one followed by 15 zeros (in the short scale) or 24 zeros (in the long scale).

- **Excogitate** ex·cog·i·tate (verb)
  Think out, plan, or devise.

- **Euouae** eu·ou·ae (noun)
  A medieval musical term.

- **Plethora** pleth·o·ra (noun)
  An excessive amount or number.

- **Garrulous** gar·ru·lous (adjective)
  Excessively talkative, especially on trivial matters.

- **Homogeneous** ho·mo·ge·ne·ous (adjective)
  Of the same kind; alike.

# LEVEL 9

- **Philanthropic** phi·lan·throp·ic (adjective)
  Seeking to promote the welfare of others, especially by donating money to good causes.

- **Exacerbate** ex·ac·er·bate (verb)
  Make (a problem, bad situation, or negative feeling) worse.

- **Grandiloquent** gran·di·lo·quent (adjective)
  Pompous or extravagant in language, style, or manner.

- **Impecunious** im·pe·cu·ni·ous (adjective)
  Having little or no money.

- **Intransigent** in·tran·si·gent (adjective)
  Unwilling or refusing to change one's views or to agree about something.

- **Multidimensional**
  mul·ti·di·men·sion·al (adjective)
  Having or involving several dimensions.

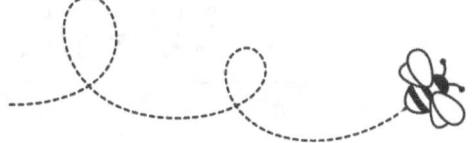

- **Noninstitutionalized**
  non·in·sti·tu·tion·al·ized (adjective)
  Not committed or confined to an institution.

- **Deleterious** de·le·te·ri·ous (adjective)
  Causing harm or damage.

- **Ytterbium** yt·ter·bi·um (noun)
  The chemical element of atomic number 70, a soft silvery-white metal of the lanthanide series.

## Bonus Words:

- **Equanimity** e·quan·im·i·ty (noun)
  Mental calmness, composure, and evenness of temper.

- **Quasiparticle** qua·si·par·ti·cle (noun)
  A disturbance in a medium that behaves as if it were a particle.

# LEVEL 10

- **Anthropomorphization**
  an·thro·po·mor·phi·za·tion (noun)
  the attribution of human characteristics or behavior
  to a god, animal, or object.

- **Bioluminescence** bio·lu·mi·nes·cence (noun)
  the biochemical emission of light by living
  organisms such as fireflies and deep-sea fishes.

- **Circumnavigation** cir·cum·nav·i·ga·tion (noun)
  the action or process of sailing or otherwise
  traveling all the way around something, especially
  the world.

- **Deoxyribonucleic** de·ox·y·ri·bo·nu·cle·ic (noun)
  Of or relating to the deoxyribonucleic acid, a
  self-replicating material present in nearly all living
  organisms as the main constituent of chromosomes.
  It is the carrier of genetic information.

- **Immunocompromised**
  im·mu·no·com·pro·mised (adjective)
  having an impaired immune system.

- **Fluorocarbon** flu·o·ro·car·bon (noun)
  Any of a class of compounds of carbon, hydrogen, chlorine, and fluorine, typically gases used in refrigerants and aerosol propellants. They are harmful to the ozone layer in the earth's atmosphere owing to the release of chlorine atoms on exposure to ultraviolet radiation.

- **Gastroenterologist** gas·tro·en·ter·ol·o·gist (noun)
  A medical practitioner with special training in the management of diseases of the gastrointestinal tract and liver.

- **Laryngopharyngeal**
  lar·yn·go·pha·ryn·ge·al (adjective)
  Relating to the larynx and the pharynx.

- **Consanguineous** con·san·guin·e·ous (adjective)
  Of the same lineage or origin; having a common ancestor.

- **Pulchritudinous** pul·chri·tu·di·nous (adjective)
  Beautiful.

# LEVEL 10

- **Nanotechnology** nan·o·tech·nol·o·gy (noun)
  The branch of technology that deals with dimensions and tolerances of less than 100 nanometers, especially the manipulation of individual atoms and molecules.

- **Transubstantiate** tran·sub·stan·ti·ate (verb)
  Change (the bread and wine used in the eucharist) into the body and blood of Christ.

- **Uncomprehendingly**
  un·com·pre·hend·ing·ly (adverb)
  In a manner that shows a lack of understanding or knowledge.

- **Trichotillomania** tricho·til·lo·ma·nia (noun)
  A compulsive desire to pull out one's hair.

- **Embourgeoisement**
  em·bour·geoi·se·ment (noun)
  The process by which bourgeois aspirations are supposedly disseminated in society.

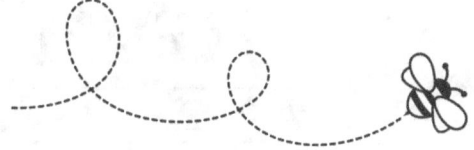

- **Whippoorwill** whip·poor·will (noun)
A nocturnal bird of the nightjar family with a distinctive, repetitive call.

- **Xenotransplantation**
xe·no·trans·plan·ta·tion (noun)
The process of grafting or transplanting organs or tissues between members of different species.

- **Myrmecophilous** myr·me·co·phil·ous (adjective)
Living in symbiosis with ants.

- **Antidisestablishmentarianism**
an·ti·dis·es·tab·lish·men·tar·i·an·ism (noun)
A political position that originated in 19th-century Britain opposing proposals for the disestablishment of the Church of England.

- **Floccinaucinihilipilification**
floc·ci·nau·ci·ni·hil·i·pil·i·fi·ca·tion (noun)
The action or habit of estimating something as worthless.

# LEVEL 10

●●●●●●●●●●

- **Conceptualization** con·cep·tu·al·i·za·tion (noun)
  The action or process of forming a concept or idea of something.

- **Tergiversation** ter·gi·ver·sa·tion (noun)
  Evasion of straightforward action or clear-cut statement.

- **Electroencephalography**
  e·lec·tro·en·ce·pha·log·ra·phy (noun)
  The measurement of electrical activity in different parts of the brain and the recording of such activity as a visual trace.

- **Gastroesophageal**
  gas·tro·e·soph·a·ge·al (adjective)
  Relating to both the stomach and the oesophagus.

- **Hydrochlorofluorocarbon**
  hy·dro·chlo·ro·flu·o·ro·car·bon (noun)
  Any of several organic compounds composed of hydrogen, chlorine, fluorine, and carbon.

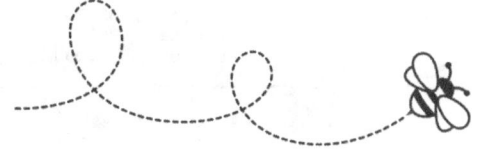

- **Anachronistic** an·ach·ro·nis·tic (adjective)
Belonging to a period other than that being portrayed.

- **Kleptocracy** klep·toc·ra·cy (noun)
A society whose leaders make themselves rich and powerful by stealing from the rest of the people.

- **Lepidopterology** lep·i·dop·ter·ol·o·gy (noun)
The branch of entomology concerning the scientific study of moths and the three superfamilies of butterflies.

- **Justiciability** jus·ti·ci·a·bil·i·ty (noun)
The quality of being subject to examination in a court of justice.

- **Palaeoanthropological**
pa·le·o·an·thro·po·log·i·cal (adjective)
Pertaining to the study of ancient humans as found in fossil hominid evidence.

# LEVEL 10

- **Accoutrements** ac·cou·tre·ments (noun)
  Additional items of dress or equipment, or other items carried or worn by a person.

- **Reconceptualization**
  re·con·cep·tu·al·i·za·tion (noun)
  The act of conceptualizing something differently or anew.

- **Transmogrification** trans·mog·ri·fi·ca·tion (noun)
  The process of transformation, particularly in a surprising or magical manner.

- **Honorificabilitudinitatibus**
  hon·or·if·ic·a·bil·i·tu·di·ni·tat·i·bus (noun)
  Being able to receive honors.

- **Whatchamacallit** what·cha·ma·call·it (noun)
  A thing whose name one has forgotten, does not know, or does not wish to mention.

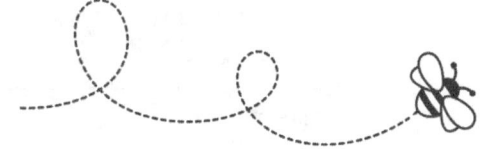

- **Vitriolic** vi·tri·ol·ic (adjective)
  Filled with bitter criticism or malice.

- **Autotransplantation**
  au·to·trans·plan·ta·tion (noun)
  The transplantation of tissues or organs from one
  part of a person's body to another.

- **Subdermatoglyphic**
  sub·der·ma·to·glyph·ic (noun)
  The ability of a substance to be decomposed by
  bacteria or other living organisms.

- **Sesquipedalian** ses·qui·pe·da·lian (adjective)
  Polysyllabic; long.

- **Electromechanically**
  e·lec·tro·me·chan·i·cal·ly (adverb)
  Involving both electrical and mechanical processes.

# LEVEL 10

- **Ferroelectricity** fer·ro·e·lec·tric·i·ty (noun)
  A characteristic of certain materials that have a spontaneous electric polarization that can be reversed by the application of an external electric field.

- **Psychotomimetic** psycho·to·mi·met·ic (adjective)
  Producing effects that mimic psychosis or a psychotic episode.

- **Incomprehensibility**
  in·com·pre·hen·si·bil·i·ty (noun)
  The quality of being impossible to understand.

- **Perspicacious** per·spi·ca·cious (adjective)
  Having a ready insight into and understanding of things.

- **Fluoroquinolone** flu·o·ro·quin·o·lone (noun)
  Any of a group of broad-spectrum antibiotics that have a bicyclic core structure related to the substance nalidixic acid.

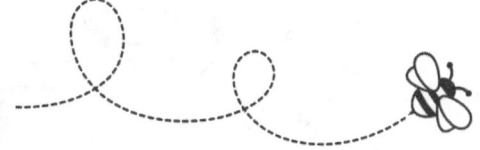

- **Preponderance** pre·pon·der·ance (noun)
  The quality or fact of being greater in number, quantity, or importance.

- **Vituperate** vi·tu·per·ate (verb)
  To blame or insult someone in strong or violent language.

- **Glottochronology** glot·to·chron·ol·o·gy (noun)
  A statistical method of dating linguistic changes by studying the rate at which words are replaced in a language.

- **Xylopyrography** xy·lo·py·rog·ra·phy (noun)
  The art of burning designs on wood or leather with a heated instrument.

- **Sesquicentennial** ses·qui·cen·ten·nial (noun)
  A one-hundred-and-fiftieth anniversary.

- **Xylophilous** xy·lo·phil·ous (adjective)
  Attracted to or living in or on wood.

# LEVEL 10

●●●●●●●●●●●

- **Triskaidekaphobia**
  tris·kai·dek·a·pho·bi·a (noun)
  Fear of the number 13.

- **Fundamentalism** fun·da·men·tal·ism (noun)
  A form of a religion, especially Islam or Protestant
  Christianity, that upholds belief in the strict, literal
  interpretation of scripture.

- **Anthropocentrism** an·thro·po·cen·trism (noun)
  Belief that human beings are the most significant
  entity of the universe.

- **Electrophoresis** e·lec·tro·pho·re·sis (noun)
  The movement of charged particles in a fluid or gel
  under the influence of an electric field.

- **Neurophysiologist**
  neu·ro·phys·i·ol·o·gist (noun)
  A health-care professional who studies the functions
  of the nervous system.

- **Otorhinolaryngology**
  o·to·rhino·lar·yn·gol·o·gy (noun)
  The study of diseases of the ear, nose, and throat.

- **Psychophysiological**
  psy·cho·phys·i·o·log·i·cal (adjective)
  Of or relating to the interrelation of physiological processes and behavior.

## Bonus Words:

- **Dichlorodiphenyltrichloroethane**
  di·chlo·ro·di·phen·yl·tri·chloro·eth·ane (noun)
  A colorless, tasteless, and almost odorless crystalline organochlorine known for its insecticidal properties.

- **Pseudopseudohypoparathyroidism**
  pseudo·pseu·do·hy·po·pa·ra·thy·roid·ism (noun)
  A condition that closely resembles pseudohypoparathyroidism but without the abnormal levels of calcium and phosphate in the blood.

# TWO**RAVENS**
### B O O K S

## Collectible imprints
## for little learners & readers

### Xander & Rem
#### Children's Coloring & Activity Books

### Xander's Perch
#### CHILDREN'S FICTION BOOKS

### Two Little Ravens
#### CHILDREN'S NON-FICTION BOOKS

# Hello Brilliant Little Explorer and Grown-Up Guide!

Thanks for embarking on the fun-filled educational journey in this book.

If you have ideas to make this book more helpful for you and others, don't hesitate to email us at **hello@ tworavensbooks.com.**

If your funny bone was tickled and your brain ignited by this adventure, we'd be delighted if you could share your giggles and gains by reviewing **A Difficult Spelling Book For Smart Kids.**

Your feedback not only helps others find this book but also fuels us to keep weaving humor and knowledge into more wonderful titles.

Keep laughing, keep learning, and thank you for your support of **Two Little Ravens**, an imprint of **Two Ravens Books LLC.**

Find more humorously educational books like this at TwoRavensBooks.com